D1223933

Pebble® Plus

Science and Engineering Practices

ASKING QUESTIONS
AND FINDING SOLUTIONS

by Riley Flynn

CAPSTONE PRESS

a capstone imprint

Pebble Plus is published by Capstone Press,
1710 Roe Crest Drive, North Mankato, Minnesota 56003
www.mycapstone.com

Copyright © 2017 by Capstone Press, a Capstone imprint. All rights reserved. No part of this publication may be reproduced in whole or in part, or stored in a retrieval system, or transmitted in any form or by any means, electronic, mechanical, photocopying, recording, or otherwise, without written permission of the publisher.

Library of Congress Cataloging-in-Publication Data
Cataloging-in-Publication data is on file with the Library of Congress.
ISBN 978-1-5157-0947-3 (library binding)
ISBN 978-1-5157-0979-4 (paperback)
ISBN 978-1-5157-1114-8 (eBook PDF)

Editorial Credits
Anna Butzer, editor; Sarah Bennett, designer; Eric Gohl, media researcher; Laura Manthe, production specialist

Photo Credits
iStockphoto: Pamela Moore, 19; Shutterstock: Annette Shaff, 7, Maxim Khytra, 20, pavla, 17, Photology1971, 11, rck_953, 5, sabzaa, 13, science photo, 15, wavebreakmedia, cover, 9

Design Elements: Shutterstock

Note to Parents and Teachers

The Science and Engineering Practices set supports Next Generation Science Standards related to Science and Engineering Practices. This book describes and illustrates asking questions and finding solutions. The images support early readers in understanding the text. The repetition of words and phrases helps early readers learn new words. This book also introduces early readers to subject-specific vocabulary words, which are defined in the Glossary section. Early readers may need assistance to read some words and to use the Table of Contents, Glossary, Read More, Internet Sites, Critical Thinking Using the Common Core, and Index sections of the book.

Printed and bound in China.
007714

Table of Contents

Why We Ask Questions

In science we ask many questions. Why is the sky blue? How do birds fly? The questions we ask help us learn more about the world.

Curiosity Is Important

A curious person asks questions
and looks for answers. Why do
dogs pant? Why do rabbits
hop? Curiosity helps us learn.

You toss a paper airplane into the air. It crashes to the ground. What went wrong? Are its wings the wrong shape? Asking questions can help solve a problem.

Observations and Answers

To find an answer, you
must first observe the problem.
Your bike isn't working.
It's hard to pedal. Can you
see the problem?

Look closely at your bike. You
see a flat tire. That's the problem.
How do you solve the problem?
You must replace the tire!

Experiments and Answers

Scientists use experiments to help answer questions. An experiment is a test that has been carefully planned. They observe what happens during an experiment.

Does wood sink in water? Do rocks float? You can find the answer by doing an experiment. Test what happens by placing these objects in water.

Look around you. Many things you use began as experiments. People saw problems. They worked to solve them. It may have taken many experiments.

Finding Answers

How much of your favorite beverage is in a glass filled with ice?

What You Need:

- drinking glass
- water
- 2-cup (475-milliliters) measuring container, marked with ounces (mL)
- washable marker
- small blocks or rocks

What You Do:

1. Fill the drinking glass with water. Then pour the water into the measuring container.

2. With the marker, draw a line along the water level. Empty the container.

3. Carefully place small blocks or rocks in the bottom of the drinking glass. These represent ice cubes.

4. Fill the glass with water. Then pour the water into the measuring container.

5. Remove the blocks or rocks.

6. Mark the water level with the marker.

7. Find the difference between the two lines. Use subtraction.

Glossary

curious—eager to explore and learn about new things

experiment—a scientific test to find out how something works

observe—to watch someone or something closely in order to learn something

problem—something that causes trouble

replace—to take the place of

solve—to find the answer to a problem

Read More

Nagelhout, Ryan. *Discovering STEM at the Baseball Game.* STEM in the Real World. New York: PowerKids Press, 2016.

Rompella, Natalie. *Experiments in Material and Matter with Toys and Everyday Stuff.* Fun Science. North Mankato, Minn.: Capstone Press, 2016.

Internet Sites

FactHound offers a safe, fun way to find Internet sites related to this book. All of the sites on FactHound have been researched by our staff.

Here's all you do:
Visit www.facthound.com
Type in this code: 9781515709473

Check out projects, games and lots more at
www.capstonekids.com

Critical Thinking Using the Common Core

1. What is an experiment? (Key Ideas and Details)

2. Why is it important for you to ask questions?
   (Integration of Knowledge and Ideas)

Index